You
you
next step beyond yourself.

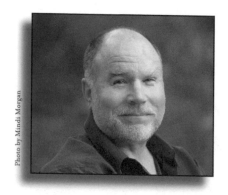

Guy Finley is a best-selling author and self-realization teacher known for his kindness, passion, and deep understanding of the interior path. He lives and teaches in Merlin, Oregon. To learn more about Guy and his life-changing ideas, visit his award-winning website at guyfinley.org.

Guy Finley has helped millions live fuller, more peaceable lives.
—BARNES AND NOBLE

Wisdom from the
* INTERNATIONAL BESTSELLER *
The Secret of Letting Go

LETTING GO

A Little Bit at a Time

GUY FINLEY

LLEWELLYN PUBLICATIONS ❧ Woodbury, Minnesota

FIRST EDITION
First Printing, 2009

Book design by Rebecca Zins
Cover design by Lisa Novak
Cover image by imagenair/PunchStock
Excerpted from *The Secret of Letting Go*
(Llewellyn, 2007) by Guy Finley

For interior photo credits, see last page

Library of Congress Cataloging-in-Publication Data
Finley, Guy, 1949-
    Letting go : a little bit at a time / Guy Finley.—1st ed.
      p. cm.
    ISBN 978-0-7387-1432-5
    1. Self-actualization (Psychology) 2. Happiness. I. Title.
BF637.S4F5555 2009
158.1—dc22

2008035543

LLEWELLYN PUBLICATIONS
2143 Wooddale Drive, Dept. 978-0-7387-1432-5
Woodbury, MN 55125-2989

WWW.LLEWELLYN.COM

Printed in the United States of America
on recycled paper

INTRODUCTION

A young man decided to visit a certain part of a distant country known for its community of uniquely gifted artists. In truth, he felt compelled to go.

Over the last few years, a growing sense of feeling strangely incomplete seemed to stalk him in spite of his many achievements. He felt blocked in some mysterious way, making him feel more like a captive in his own life than the captain of it. And so ... the unspoken hope behind his journey was to find someone, something, to help him release the great but still latent forces he knew lived in his heart. He longed to free himself from what he sensed was keeping him from being able to express his True Self...

Soon after settling in at a small hostel for budget-minded travelers, he found himself out walking through an expansive outdoor bazaar where hundreds of local artisans displayed their works. However, despite the colorful character of the place and its highly animated people, he couldn't hide the growing sense of disappointment descending on him. Nothing he saw moved him; everything seemed commonplace, just another dead end. What now?

He kept on walking without even noticing that the hustle and bustle of the bazaar was now far behind him. And that's when something happened that would forever change his life, although he couldn't know it at the moment.

He was so wrapped up in his own thoughts about all the wasted years spent searching for some silly "secret," it's a wonder he heard anything at all, but just then his ear caught the slightly ringing sound of someone tapping, rapping lightly on something from just on the other side of an old wooden fence. He tried to look through it, but no luck. A moment later, after turning a corner in the fence that lined the cobbled street, he came upon an open gate; he peered inside, taking care not to be seen by whoever was working there.

He was surprised to see a rather small young woman seated there, in an open courtyard, surrounded by dozens of stones of all shapes and sizes. Her features were soft, and a faded red scarf was tied around her auburn hair.

Set all around her—some on tables, with others freestanding behind her—were various stone sculptures of wild animals, mostly great birds. And though it was obvious these creations were still in various stages of completion, they already exuded a presence that almost pulled him out of his hiding spot and into the courtyard. "What have I stumbled onto here?" he mused to himself, leaning in a little farther to see what else he could.

Just then the young lady stood up, wiped her hands on her work apron, and walked toward one of the larger, darker stones that was perched on a work pedestal of some kind. She moved slowly around it, studying something, until she pulled a little hammer of some sort from out of her apron pocket. He leaned in a little farther still, not wanting to miss whatever was to happen next.

After a further careful examination of one small area on the face of the dark stone set there before her, she rapped it—just once—with her small hammer. She used so little force that he felt sorry for her timidity. Surely, he thought, she must be a novice of some kind—but his eyes couldn't believe what happened next.

As soon as her tap was delivered, dozens of small pieces of the stone broke away, showering the ground with dark fragments. At first he thought she had made a mistake and had cracked the whole stone; a moment later, he knew otherwise. She had not ruined the stone; instead, somehow, she had released its secret character.

With that one careful tap, she brought into the light not only a beautiful, white marble-like material, but she had somehow managed to shape the newly revealed stone to resemble the graceful neck of a great swan. He was stunned. What magic was this? His longing to know swept away any concern that he might be seen as an intruder, and he walked into the courtyard, saying "Hello!"

"Hello to you!" she responded in a bright, welcoming voice, seemingly unsurprised by his out-of-the-blue entrance.

"Please forgive me," he went on, "but I was just outside the gate when I couldn't help see what just happened here. How in the world did you do that with a single blow from your tiny hammer?" He was pointing toward the sculpture of the emerging swan, but she already knew what he meant.

"Oh," she said, laughing out loud. "I didn't see you there, but I'm guessing you only watched me work for a few minutes before I struck that last blow, yes?"

"Yes," he said, "that's right," nodding his head in agreement. "But still ... that doesn't really explain ..."

She interrupted him. "It does, you see, but only once you understand that before you began watching me just now, I had delivered hundreds of similar small blows to the exact same spot on that stone. What you just witnessed was the result of many days of careful work coupled with a special kind of quiet consideration."

Sensing his disbelief at how she was able to strike such a deft blow with seemingly no effort on her part, she continued. "Yes, that's right," her eyes smiled at him, letting him know he was about to be told a great secret, "That's how all great things are achieved: consistent attention coupled with persistent effort—a little bit at a time—until the right time comes when that work is rewarded."

She looked at him for a moment to see if he had understood. His quiet smile said yes, so she finished her thought.

"Then nothing can stand in the way of what must be released. The practice of this knowledge, in whatever one intends to do, must produce a subsequent revelation that is the heart of liberation itself."

They shared one more smile between them in the kind of silence that only close friends enjoy. Then they shook hands and said goodbye.

With consistent attention and persistent effort, you can release whatever now stands between you and the freedom for which your heart seeks. You can let go. Never mind what's happened in the past; forget whatever your mind tells you can't be done. You don't need strength or even courage to drop those dark thoughts and feelings that have your heart and mind tied down; all you need to shatter any unwanted situation is the willingness to see what's true and what's not about you.

The truth is, once you have the right interior tools and know how to use them, nothing in the universe can stop you from breaking out of old patterns and starting life over.

This book is filled with hundreds of powerful, small "hammers"—special insights on exactly when and where to apply the liberating light of higher self-awareness—so that, a little at a time, you're empowered to strike the gentle interior blows that release the truly free and fearless you.

Now, all that's left to do—to start a whole new chapter of your life—is to turn the page and welcome the light that first reveals and then releases you to realize your highest possibilities.

Guy Finley

We struggle with whatever we do—with whatever personally compromises us or our contentment in life—so that we might realize a greater measure of freedom.

When it comes to letting go and growing beyond who and what we have been up until that time, the deal is non-negotiable: first comes our gradual awakening to what no longer works for us, followed by the inner work to release the same. Then, and only then, dawns the discovery and realization of what is—in all cases—a new and higher order of our self; our life is transformed.

In one hand, there is the "rock" of
not wanting to go through what we
know must be done; in the other
is "the hard place" of seeing that
no other options are available.

Ask yourself what happens to
a kite when its string is cut.
Up it goes! It climbs into the
open skies above it because
that's its nature; it was
made to rise. So are we:
we are made to be free.

We each have—right here, right now—everything we need to succeed with finding the lasting wholeness and happiness for which our heart of hearts seeks.

Our problem is that we're sure we have to do something to be free. Strangely enough, the only thing between us and a life without limits is this mistaken idea.

Freedom from the burden of false
responsibilities ... real reconciliation
with lovers, friends, and family ... the
grace to forgive old foes completely ...
a growing sense of a loving and
compassionate intelligence unbound
by passing time: these gifts and more
come to those who learn to let go.

Think of letting go as learning
to take part in the breath of
life itself, something that is as
natural to who you truly are
as it is for the sun to shine.

The divine intelligence that seeded
within you the wish to realize a
free, holy, fearless life will see
to its flowering, providing you
nourish this same wish with all
your heart, mind, and soul.

Our greatest strength isn't our ability to imagine brighter days ahead, it is that we are empowered—in every present moment—to effortlessly dismiss any dark thought or feeling that, left unattended, diminishes our happiness.

This True Self—the secret heart
of your soul—always remains
open and responsive and never
holds on to any position other
than the wish to learn what
is true. This is its power.

This new relationship with your self
will keep you safe and inspired forever.
With each new insight you gain about
your true nature, your life-level
automatically rises. To your endless
delight, you will discover that each
higher view is more inspiring than the
last, and this will encourage you to keep
climbing in order to see more. This
magical kind of relationship in life
does exist. It's yours for the asking.

Nothing in the universe can
stop you from letting go and
starting over. *Nothing*.

Your True Self can no more
get "stuck" somewhere than
a beam of sunlight can be
held down by a shadow.

Real change itself isn't found
in some new way to think
about yourself but in the
freedom from the need to
think about yourself at all.

The fact is a new life does exist;
you need only search for it in
the right place. When standing
over a buried treasure, you need
only dig until you find it.

Defeat is a memory; it does
not exist in real life.

Letting go has nothing to do
with the release of anything
outside of yourself.

We have been living from an
unseen part of ourselves: a self
that thinks clinging to wreckage
is the same as being rescued!

We must let go of this sorry
self that is certain it is better to
suffer and *feel* like someone than
it is to just let go and quietly *be*
no one. Have no concerns how
this task will be accomplished.
That is reality's responsibility.

This higher knowledge that is now beginning to reveal you to yourself is *not* mental. It is coming to you from a lofty, wise, and powerful part of yourself that lives way above everyday thinking and its ceaseless conflict over what may or may not be best.

You don't need to ache, even
when you are sure you must.

The secret of letting go not only holds the keys for ending what is unwanted, but locked within this same supreme secret is the beginning of your new life—the birth of a new nature that never has to hold on to anything because it is *already everything*.

Uncovering what is wrong
must always precede the
discovery of what is right.

Letting go is strictly
an inside job.

You can never act any higher
toward a situation than your
understanding of that situation.

Letting go is the natural release
that always follows the realization
that holding on hurts.

Unhappiness does not come
at you, it comes from you.

Letting go happens effortlessly once
you see there is no other choice.

Real freedom is the absence
of the self that feels trapped,
not the trappings that self
acquires to make it feel free.

Wanting to learn about yourself
while limiting your discoveries
to what you want to find is
like saying "I want to see the
whole world from my bed."

The only thing you lose when you
let go of something you are afraid
to live without is the fear itself.

There is a way past this part of yourself that would rather hold on than get out. However, to really let go of these fears, we must first go through them.

The seemingly scary condition, whatever it may be, is not the problem. It is your *reaction* that is fearful. This is why if you will become *conscious* of your condition instead of afraid of it, you will change forever your relationship with fear.

Each day, as you discover
something new about the strange
and shaky nature of your own
fearful reactions, they begin to
lose their power over you. Why?
Because you are at last seeing them
for what they have always been:
unintelligent mechanical forces.

To be consciously afraid means
that you know you are frightened,
but at the same time you know
that these very fears, as real as
they may seem, are not you.

Fear is, and has always been, nothing
but a self-limiting reaction that we
cling to in the darkness of our present
life-level, having mistaken it for a
shield of self-protection. But, just as
the faintest of early morning sunlight
can dispel the night-long darkness,
so does the smallest of insights into a
persistent fear lead to letting it go.

Dare to proceed even while being afraid. But remember, your new aim isn't to be courageous or to try and act strong in the face of fear. No. We've seen that this won't work. You simply want to be more curious about your frightened thoughts and feelings than you want to believe in them.

Almost every kind of unhappy
feeling is the result of mistaking
the partial for the whole.

We are wrongly led to believe
that life makes us into the kind
of person we are. The truth is
that the kind of person we
are—our life-level—makes
life what it is for us!

You can let go of those resentful
feelings toward your job,
because the treadmill isn't
what you are doing but the
way you are thinking.

You can let go of trying to change
other people, because *you* are what
is bothering you about them.

You can let go of the fear
of unforeseen changes or
challenges, because all you
really ever have to face in any
challenging moment is yourself.

Best of all, you can let go of the impossible and unbelievably self-punishing task of thinking that you are responsible for the way the world turns. The only world you are responsible for is your inner world: the world of your thoughts and feelings, impulses and desires.

Do not try to change the external
world. Change your own attitudes
and viewpoints. When you change
yourself, you change the world
as far as you are concerned,
for you are your own world.

Trying to change your life without
first changing your life-level is like
trying to convince yourself that
a Ferris wheel has a destination.
If you are tired of going around
and around, remember that you
can get off whenever you choose.

Any human being who has to
hold himself together is someone
who is ready to fall apart.

Being unhappy over being unhappy
is like throwing gasoline on a
fire to put it out: you get lots of
fire and smoke—even a strange
excitement—but in the end,
all you are left with is ashes.

You can make yourself miserable,
but you can't make yourself happy.

You could never be unhappy
with anything you found in
this life if you didn't already
have it fixed in your mind
what you were looking for.

Happiness isn't something that
can be made. It isn't the result
of anything. Happiness comes to
those who understand that you
can't seek it any more than you seek
the air you breathe. It is a part of
life to be found within living.

All pursuit of happiness is based
upon the false assumption
that there is a way to possess
it; you may as well try to
grab a handful of breeze!

Happiness is the natural expression
of a stress-free life, just as
sunlight naturally warms the earth
after dark clouds disappear.

FEBRUARY 23

Face fear's full bluff.

54

Happiness is letting go of your
ideas about happiness.

Let go of all the familiar but
useless rules of rigor that tell
you life would be meaningless
without running around in
some kind of conflict.

Letting go of what holds you down
is how you cooperate with going
up. You see, your true nature
is high. And this is your new
destination. But *you* don't choose
it. No. You allow yourself to rise.

Walking away from what is
false is the same as heading
toward what is true.

The very act of doing something
for a reward is painful because
it goes against your true nature,
which is a reward unto itself.

Whatever we are driven to win
can never lead to true victory,
because anyone who is driven
to do anything is being whipped
along by forces outside of
himself. This is the definition
of a slave, not a conqueror.

Suffering now so that you can
be happy in the future makes as
much sense as throwing yourself
overboard so that later you can
feel relief about being rescued.

Any want that is compulsive
can never be a source of real
pleasure, since anything you
are compelled to want makes
you a servant of that very drive.
There is very little pleasure in
being pushed through life.

Learn to listen to any feelings that
cast doubt on your need to suffer.

Asking to see more about a
painful situation is the same as
asking how you can let it go.

Walking away from the
problems you don't want in
your life gets easier each time
it becomes clearer to you who
you no longer need to be.

You are not who you think you are.
This is one of the most exciting
and relief-filled self-findings
you can make about yourself.

By placing ourselves in the care
of real intelligence, we can learn
to let go of whatever it may be
that has frightened us up to now.
That's right. The winds of this
world can blow hot or cold, gently
or in gales, and it won't matter to
you. You have found yourself.

Looking for yourself outside of yourself—whether through career, hobbies, or in the faces of people, family, or strangers—is like trying to find your reflection in a tumbling mountain brook.

Events may happen to you,
but you are not the event.

Those who don't know their
true identity do not know that
they don't know who they are.

We are deceived whenever we
find ourselves feverishly thinking
through "all the possibilities"
stirred up by a fearful moment,
because the only possibility *any*
of these fearful thoughts hold
is which one of them is about
to make us its prisoner.

There is no profit in blaming your unhappiness on other people or an uncaring world. This is the solution the false self wants you to embrace, because it knows that if it can get you to see life its way, then you will have no choice but to spend the rest of your life struggling with conditions outside of yourself. This is its conquest.

Own your own life.

No negative state is interested
in ending itself.

The false self can throw terrifying
shadows, but now you can cast
inner light. There is no contest.

Mountains crumble in the
presence of those who know
how to wait, watch, and then
boldly walk through the passage
that appears before them.

In our battle with the false self,
we defeat it not by running away
or through struggle with it, but
by standing still long enough
to see that we have mistakenly
attributed power to it.

The only power the false self
has over us is that we still find
pleasure living under it.

The more the false self can clash
with reality, the more alive it feels.

Feeling like someone special
because others or events have lifted
you is like living in a sandcastle that
was built for you at water's edge.

Losing is the false self's idea
of winning, which is why
it looks forward to fighting
with reality every day.

If life knocks you flat on
your back, open your eyes:
above you are the stars.

We would never tolerate a
dictatorial government, so
why do we put up with all of
the inner tyrants—including
their leader, the chief dictator,
better known as the false self?

When you learn to think about your thinking, this special kind of self-separation allows you to question its intelligence.

Saying yes when you mean to say no, or vice versa, is a small but painful illustration of what happens to us when we don't examine our thoughts and feelings before speaking. Resentment almost always follows.

The false self loves
to feel resentful.

Just as you would never buy a
sack of diamonds without first
confirming the seller's professional
standing and the stones' actual
value, you should never buy any of
your own thoughts or feelings until
you are certain of their source—
and that they are, indeed, yours!

Somehow we have become
separated from the real
intelligence within us that knows
better than to punish itself.

Your feelings, good or bad, are
not the masters of your life; they
are merely moments within it.

You break free of unhappy
thoughts and emotions by seeing
that, even though it may feel
that way at the moment, you are
not owned by them. You are
only temporarily occupied.

As you come to own yourself,
which is the sole purpose of this
life, it becomes impossible to ever
think or feel that you are owned
by anything or anyone else.

The false self is nothing more than
a shadow that can throw its voice.

The illusion of feeling useless
or otherwise insignificant in
life—with its heartache and
sorrow—is born of the false
perception that the true measure
of your worth is determined
by what others agree it to be.

The illusion of discouragement—
with its bitterness and blame—is
born of the false perception that it's
possible to succeed in life without
learning through your "failures."

The illusion of regret—with
its seemingly inescapable grief
and guilt—is born of the false
perception that by reliving some
past painful moment, you will
be empowered to resolve it.

The illusion of limitation—with
its fear and sense of frustration—is
born of the false perception that
the only resource available to
you in the moment of challenge
is what you already know as
being possible for you to do.

The illusion that others are
better, stronger, or wiser than you
are—with its painful self-doubt
and insecurity—is born of the false
perception that you are here on
earth to be like someone else.

Self-observation allows us to
understand what we witness in
ourselves, instead of being washed
away by our reaction to it.

The silent observer within
us does not think; it sees.

The only thing valuable about
any fearful state is seeing how
worthless it really is and then—
along with the false self that loves
to scare itself—just letting it go.

Remember, light need never
fear any shadow, and anything
you may discover within you
that is frightening comes from
the shadow world. Your only
task is to bring it into the light
of your new understanding,
and let it handle the rest.

Once you get the feel for it,
self-observation is no more difficult
than leisurely watching a juggler under
the big top. He may have as many as
six or seven assorted objects flipping
and spinning all at once, but that is *of
no concern to you.* Seeing takes no effort;
you are just enjoying the performance!

The only work we do of lasting
value is the work that we do for
ourselves within ourselves.

We have a definite conditioned dependency to think of things as worthwhile only if someone else recognizes their value. This painful kind of thinking not only leaves us trying to please others, but it also discourages us from embarking upon the exciting journey of self-investigation.

In our appearance-oriented thinking, we wrongly believe that unless someone else can see our inner efforts or in some way approve our self-discoveries, our work has been in vain. Nothing could be further from the truth.

Your True Self is pleasing to itself and
so needs nothing outside of its own
elevated state in order to feel successful.
This exalted inner condition, which
is the source of true self-liberation,
already lives within you. It is not
something that you need to add to
yourself, since it has always belonged
to you. This special knowledge teaches
us that this greatest of all prizes is a
realization and not an acquisition.

You must learn to stop
thinking in terms of
beginnings and endings,
successes and failures,
and begin to treat
everything in your life
as a *learning* experience
instead of a *proving* one.

The highest peaks of great
mountains almost always have
banks of dark clouds resting just
beneath them. You must climb
through these clouds in order to
conquer the heights. Then the
higher view belongs to you.

You don't need to be strong,
only willing to see. If you will
do your part, which is to reveal
you to yourself, your higher
nature will provide you with
all the strength you need.

Learning is a correction process.
Real correction, at any level,
always purifies the matter
and so leaves it less confused
and thus in a higher state.

With self-correction, we *learn*
for ourselves that we have been
teaching ourselves incorrectly.

As we experience the benefits
of letting go of ourselves,
vigorous new inner growth
then takes place as naturally as
it does for a young plant that
has been moved from a shadowy
place out into the sunlight.

Learning can only take place
outside the shadow of pride.
Anything that resists correction
is a part of what is wrong.

Pride is the middle name of the false self. It is this false nature of ours that always leaps to defend itself when confronted with any kind of meaningful correction.

Remember, this lower nature is happy with its current disorderly existence. You lose when it wins, and it wins by getting you to deny or protect your mistake. Denying any problem makes you its guardian and leaves you chained to being wrong.

Being wrong is not the problem.
Defending the life-level that
produced the wrongness is
where we make the mistake.

You are not tied to any
past mistake unless you
lash yourself to it.

Trying to calm down a runaway negative reaction by talking to yourself about it is like whispering sweet nothings to a noisy kitchen blender, hoping it will hear you and start chopping more quietly!

By trying to hide the problem from
yourself, you shut the window
on the possibility of looking
into your current life-level,
which is the only world where
real correction can take place.

Letting go is not giving
up; it is going up.

If you see you are wrong,
then at that instant you can
give up being wrong.

Giving up the painful temporary
identity of being wrong is
the same as letting go of your
lower nature, the false self.

If we will place learning before
our pleasure, one day learning
will come before our pain.

You possess a potential power that is
superior to any difficulty that life may
ever present. It makes no difference
what form the challenge may assume
or how huge it looms. This latent
power of yours can render it harmless
and ultimately make it disappear.

No human being is a victim of
any punishment outside of their
own undeveloped life-level from
which their inner reactions
are seen as outer attacks.

Each time you ask the right
question about an inner ache,
you receive the new and right
result of being released from the
dark deceptions of the false self
that wants you to fight with life.

Instead of always asking yourself
why things always happen to you,
learn to ask *What is it inside of me
that attracts these painful situations?*

Instead of always asking yourself
why things had to go this way or
that way, learn to ask *Why is the way I
feel always determined by external conditions?*

Instead of always asking
yourself how to protect yourself
in challenging situations,
learn to ask *What is it in me that
always needs to be defended?*

Instead of always asking yourself
how to clear up your mental
fog, learn to ask *Can confusion
know anything about clarity?*

Instead of always asking yourself what to do about tomorrow (or the next minute), learn to ask *Can there ever be intelligence in anxiety or worry?*

Instead of always asking yourself
why so-and-so acts this or that way,
learn to ask *What's inside of me that wants
to hurt itself over how anyone else acts?*

Instead of always crying out
"Why me?" learn to ask *Who is
this "me" that always feels this way?*

Instead of always asking yourself if you've made the right choice, learn to ask *Can fear ever make a safe decision?*

Instead of always asking yourself
why doesn't so-and-so see how
wrong they are, learn to ask
*Is what I'm feeling about that person
right now good for me? Or them?*

Instead of always asking yourself
how to get others to approve
of you, learn to ask *What do I
really want, the applause of the crowds
or to quietly have my own life?*

Seeking to comfort ourselves by
clinging to the hope of a better
time to come is like a hungry man
standing outside a restaurant,
looking in through the window
and trying to fill his empty stomach
by watching other people eat.

Real pleasure in this life comes
from knowing that you are in
command of yourself *now*.

You will never agree to spend
another moment with worried
thoughts and feelings once
you realize that they don't
care about *you* at all!

Hoping to find comfort and
life direction in your wants
is like trying to find shade
under a swarm of stinging
flies—while it may be cooler,
you also have to keep running.
Your pleasure is your pain.

Real pleasure is not the *opposite* of pain, it is the *absence* of it.

What you really want is to be free
of your wants. This higher want
becomes an answerable need
the more we realize that we do
not have to sit by and submit to
anything not of our own choosing.

No one chooses to be pulled
apart unless their idea of
happiness is going to pieces.

Our wants seem to hold the
promise of a brighter, more
pleasant future, when the truth is
that it is their very nature that is
disturbing the present moment.
Everything is pleasant *now*.

You wouldn't throw a pebble
into a pond to quiet its surface.
Left alone, the pond reflects the
heavens above it. The more we
learn to leave ourselves alone,
the clearer it becomes that we
are happier that way. No one
likes a nag, so it's no small
wonder we don't like ourselves.

The only reason your
mind won't stop its endless
chattering is because you
won't stop listening to it!

The more light we can put on
those parts of us that tell us it's
OK to wallow in dark thoughts
and feelings, the less power
they have to deceive us with
the pain they would justify.

Calling on anxious thoughts
to answer fearful feelings is
like trying to stop a landslide
by throwing rocks at it!

The more we awaken to the
realization that quiet happiness is
our true natural state, the sooner
we will recognize and release
whatever would compromise
us by sending us out to look
for what we already possess.

Nothing is more productive than
watching our own thoughts and
feelings; self-observation not
only reveals unconscious self-
wrecking states for what they
are, but this order of higher
awareness also protects us from
their wasteful negative influences.

In spite of how things may appear to us, we are never trapped by *where* we are. The trap is always *who* we are.

When you run into a personal
obstacle, you have not run into an
outer condition that is denying
you happiness. You have run into
your own present life-level.

When you hear someone say,
"I'm sick and tired of it," what
they are really saying without
realizing it is that they're sick
and tired of suffering from their
own lack of understanding.

Unhappiness does not come
at us, it comes *from* us.

We have never been trapped by
anything outside of our own lack
of understanding. This is why even
the attempt to disconnect ourselves
from the limitations of our present
life-level already belongs to a
higher level of understanding.

Persistence is everything in
your personal work. You must
persist, even if it is only with
your wish to be persistent.

The greater the doubt you will dare
to step through, the greater your
possibility to grow beyond yourself.

The only barriers between yourself
and a life without limits are the
powers you've mistakenly given
to your doubts and fears.

What is spiritual strength?
It's knowing you don't have
to compromise yourself in
any way—with anyone, over
anything—in order to be content,
confident, and secure in life.

Any thought telling you "it can't
be done" is only as convincing as
you're willing to be held captive
by its lie. Getting started—with
whatever it may be—is as simple as
remembering that there's nothing
in the universe that can stop
you from taking the first step.

Refuse to revisit your own
past for a way out of any
present problem you face.

Never explain yourself to anyone
out of fear they may misjudge you.

Learn to see your own
defensiveness toward others
as an offense against your own
right to be free of fear.

Whenever possible, realize that
the person you are about to argue
with is in as much pain as you are.

Never accept any negative reaction
you may have as the only possible
answer to your present challenge.

Remember that everything you
resist in life increases its weight by
the magnitude of thought spent in
not wanting it, so accept all that
you can and quietly drop the rest.

Common psychological suffering
is a waste of life. It is pointless,
cruel, and, above all, deceptive.

Psychological suffering is
an unnecessary pain that we
are presently certain is not
only necessary, but actually
unavoidable ... a part of "real life."

You do not have to live with any
tormenting thoughts or feelings,
no matter how compelling their
cries to convince you otherwise.

There is always a choice when it comes to psychological suffering. You need never surrender to any wave of helplessness that leaves you feeling sorry for being alive.

The desperate search for happiness is the continuation of unhappiness. Happiness is never driven to look for itself. It is itself.

Any direction we take to get
away from some misery is the
continuation of that distress, no
matter how much time and space
we may put between us and it.

Start watching yourself in action.
Here's just one example: catch yourself
listening to a familiar anxious state
telling you how to make the best plans
for a secure tomorrow—and then
ask yourself if it makes sense to ask a
shark how to get out of the ocean.

Nothing is more discontented than our lower nature, the false self. Since it has no real life of its own, it must endlessly create stimulating thoughts and feelings of one kind or another in order to give it the sensations of being alive.

The false self is desperately afraid
of not having the next thing to do,
even if it's only to suffer over not
yet having the next thing to do.

Discontentment is a kind of psychic echo. In fact, whatever the unhappiness may be, it is only an inner echo that is "sounding" within us. As difficult as it may be to understand this at the present time, suffering only *seems* real. It has no *real* life.

Our inner stress, strain, and pain feel real to us, for sure; but then, so do all of the fears we feel in the middle of a nightmare. But where is the terror once we wake up? It doesn't exist anymore because it was only real as long as we were participating in the bad dream.

The false self is trying endlessly to
get your attention in order to point
out to you that there is something
missing in your life. Who needs
a friend who wakes you up every
night to ask if you are asleep?

No self-described condition of what you have or don't have is at the root of your aching. Your feelings of discontentment and unhappiness, all of these hollow echoes, are the very nature of the false self with which you have unknowingly identified.

What is important to remember
is when something from within
you starts telling you that you are
all alone, you are not hearing
your nature but the voice of
separateness itself. This is why
you must never do anything about
your discontentment—because
it *is not your discontentment*.

Don't be afraid of not having something to do. Choose being over doing, and one day there will be no more pain in what you do or don't do, because you won't be doing anything anymore to prove to yourself that you *are* real. You are, and you will know it.

Trying to forget a fear is like trying
to hold an inflated basketball
under the water. It takes all of your
strength and attention, and in
time it must pop to the surface.

Nothing keeps us more aware of a
problem than our struggle to forget
it. Listen to what truth is trying
to tell you about your strengths
instead of listening to your
weakness tell you where to hide.

Only what is wrong with you
wants you to forget what is wrong
with you. What is right with you
knows that the only thing that
is wrong with you is that you
don't *know* what is wrong—and
that is why you stay pained.

See the upset not as an exterior
circumstance to be remedied,
but rather as an interior
condition to be understood.

Trying to change what you get from
life without first changing what you
know about life is like putting on
dry clothes over wet ones and then
wondering why you keep shivering.

The real reason people remain captives
of unwanted circumstances in their
lives is because they've yet to realize
this great spiritual secret: Resistance is
negative attraction. In other words: the
longer we dwell on what we *don't* want in
life, the larger grows that dark dwelling
place in which we find ourselves living.

Spiritual knowledge isn't something
mysterious or out of this world.
In fact, spiritual understanding is
the most important and practical
knowledge a person can possess. It
is ultimately what we know about
ourselves, about who we really are, that
determines the quality of our life.

Real strength is the refusal to act from weakness. See where you have been calling inner weakness an inner strength, such as calling anxiety concern or anger righteousness. Dare to live without these false strengths.

Have the courage to proceed even
while knowing that you are afraid.

Forgiveness is the personal
understanding that except for
circumstance there is no real
difference between you and
your offender. In spite of all the
inner screams to the contrary,
dare to treat your trespasser as
you would want to be treated.

When you stop punishing others
for their weakness, you will stop
punishing yourself for yours.

Compassion is the conscious
refusal to add to another person's
suffering, even though it may
seem to increase yours.

See that anytime you feel pained
or defeated, it is only because
you insist on clinging to what
doesn't work. Dare to let go,
and you won't lose a thing
except for a punishing idea.

No matter what the harmful
voices within may say, whoever
puts the truth first will never
lose anything except for what was
never real in the first place.

Nothing brings higher ideas
to life more strongly than your
sincere wish to understand them.

A feeling is just that—a feeling. It
has no true independent existence
for us apart from the momentary
relationship that produces it.

You will be well on your way
when your wish to remain aware
of your pleasures is stronger than
your wish to lose yourself in their
feelings. Only the awareness of
your pleasures allows you to enjoy
them without feeling as though you
are disappearing when they do.

Your true nature cannot be carried away. Whether your emotional seas blow furiously or present a picture-perfect horizon, you remain pleased because now your real pleasure is in your awareness that *you* are what is constant.

The pursuit of a pleasure to
ease a pain is like running after
a breeze to cool you down.

Trying to find pleasure in your
feelings alone is like looking
for a staircase on a rainbow.

Winning what the world has
to offer provides you with
its temporary pleasures, but
overcome the world within you
and you gain a treasure whose
permanence is timeless.

Stress exists because we insist! It's really
that simple. It is our mistaken
belief that we must push life
in the direction we choose
that keeps us in a strained and
unhappy relationship with it.

Our wish to have power over
life comes from this wrong
relationship with life. Reality
has its own effortless course, and
we can either embrace its way or
struggle endlessly with our own.
We do not need power to flow. Why push
when we can learn to ride?

There is no power on earth that
can make you feel safe and secure,
because it isn't this world that
threatens or disturbs you. You
seek worldly and personal power
because you are dominated by
your own thoughts and feelings.

What you really want is to
leave yourself alone.

Who you really are doesn't
need protection from any
event in life—regardless of how
challenging—any more than a
mountain needs a raincoat to
get through a summer storm!

Your higher, permanent nature
needs no power outside of
itself in order to be in charge
of an inner or outer attacker.

You need not answer to any
disturbance within you. Any form
of response to a negative state,
other than to silently observe it,
is always a form of resistance to
it. And what we resist persists.

You have been taught by wrong
example and false traditions that
negative thoughts and feelings
such as fear, anger, and hatred are
something you are responsible
for; that they belong to you.
You are indeed responsible
for them, but not *to* them.

Inner aches and dark feelings are
not yours. They never have been
and they never will be, no matter
how much these inner impostors
try to convince you otherwise.

I am not saying to act or pretend
as though dark feelings don't exist.
Pretending as though a rampaging
elephant isn't there or that it's a cute
bunny may feel good temporarily, but
it leaves you in danger. Seeing the
elephant and recognizing it for what it is
allows intelligence to take you where you
need to be—which is out of the jungle.

No grief or disturbance of any kind is yours. These huge inner shadows with all their howling may be present, but where is it written that they belong to you?

Whenever we seek some power
to make a fear go away, all we are
doing is empowering the fear.

The next time you feel compelled
to help yourself out of a dark
inner thought or feeling, go silent,
and watch the dark clouds of
thoughts and feelings pass through
you. Behind them is the sun.

Why is it that we will challenge
and even work to change the
world's opinions as they concern
us, but we almost never question
our own beliefs—no matter
how much stress and anxiety
they may produce within us?

What is timeless and true is
not something impractical and
hopelessly distant from us. It is as
close and immediate as our wish to
understand why it is that we keep
hurting ourselves and others.

It is what we can see *about* this
world that is our real safety,
not what we can win *from* it.

We are tied to whatever we avoid.

The more we try to become
someone special, or even seem
to succeed at the task, the
more in jeopardy we feel.

Once you know, which you
will, that you have already been
given an independent, timeless
identity, you need never worry
again about making yourself into
"someone." This is real success.

Blaming a trap that you walked
into is like getting angry at a
French fry that was too hot
to put in your mouth.

The truth is, we are never trapped
by any experience. The painful
experience of feeling trapped
is the effect of the trap, not the
trap itself. The more we try to
change the experience, the more
we unknowingly tighten the jaws
of the real inner invisible trap.

The only strength any psychological
snare may possess is in our
unawareness of its presence.

We fall into the power trap any
time we go looking for a strength
outside of ourself instead of
revealing to ourself the inner
weakness that sent us seeking.

If you are seeking power, you are
under the power of that which
has no power, and, regardless
of appearances, you will become
increasingly powerless.

Trying to arrive at true
independence by depending on
others is like trying to reach the
stars by climbing into a hole.

Unfortunately, almost all important, potentially life-changing moments are entirely missed, because what is wrong with us—our false nature—sees what is true as an attacking enemy.

Never are the healing powers
of the truth so close as
when a crisis is at hand.

A crisis always precedes any
real inner advancement,
because real spiritual growth
is a process of removing self-
blocking thoughts and feelings.

The reason a crisis must precede
each new level of authentic self-
unity is that the crisis, whatever it
may be, points out where we have
been holding on to a particular
belief, a shaky pretense, or some
flattering but deceptive self-image
that is in conflict with reality.

What we call a personal "crisis"
is really that moment when some
previously invisible conflict within
us becomes temporarily visible.

A crisis arises when some lie we
have deceived ourselves with is
revealed to be just that: a lie.

The more we take the side of
defending what is wrong within us,
the more the truth that exposed
this unconscious wrongness
appears to be against us.

The truth never causes pain. The
only pain in a crisis is the false
self's resistance to the truth.

A crisis only becomes a breaking
point when we fail to use it as
a turning point. In order to
transform a crisis into a personal
turning point in your life, you
must wish to be shown the lesson
in the crisis rather than allow
yourself to be convinced by it
that the world is against you.

Pretending that the pain has
gone away only compounds its
punishment when it returns—
which it always does, if its cause
has not been eliminated.

Everyone wonders whether or not
there is one great secret for truly
successful living. There is. And
it is not a secret. Listen quietly
for a moment: everything can
change right now. Learning to hear
this supreme secret is no more
difficult than choosing whether
to swim against a current or to let
it carry you safely to the shore.

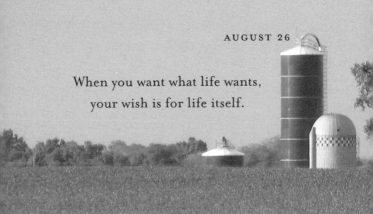

When you want what life wants,
your wish is for life itself.

Try to see that it is not what
life has brought to you that you
don't like. It is your reactions
that turn the gift of life into
the resentment of it.

Unhappy feelings are born out of
life failing to conform to your ideas
of what you need to be happy. Life
itself isn't denying you happiness.

It is *your ideas about life* that have
failed you. Give up these wrong
ideas instead of giving up on life.

To let real life flood in, pull
yourself out of the flood of self-
wants that promises a *future* pleasure
but only delivers a *present* pain.

Never accept the presence of any
mental or emotional suffering as
necessary, no matter how much
importance these impostors lend
to a particularly pressing want.

You cannot lose control of something you never had control over in the first place. No human being controls life—his or hers or anyone else's.

If you want to measure the level of
an individual's stress, measure his
insistence that life does as he wants.

The only thing you will lose by
learning to want *what life wants*
is your fear of not being in
control, which was never real
control in the first place but only
the sensation of it, born out of
living with its painful opposite.

Let life bring you itself. Welcome
it. At each instant, it is new,
full—untouched and undiminished
by any moment before it.

Nothing can be released and
resisted at the same time, which
means that any attempt to reject
some weakness detected in us
is the same as protecting it.

True nobility is not a question of
birthright or social rank, it is the
native estate of each soul that, upon
awakening to its divine inheritance,
knows the strength of these twin
truths without having to think
about them: justice and mercy are
one, as are love and fearlessness.

We can spend our time struggling,
in vain, to make others into what we
want them to be, or we can see the
inherent flaw in thinking this way,
and—rather than trying to change
others to suit our needs—see through
the false idea that someone else is
responsible for our fulfillment.

Starting life over again is the key to
a new you. Never mind all of those
thoughts and feelings that may be
telling you this is impossible—those
inner whisperings that either deny
the need for this self-newness
or that scoff at its possibility.

Self-defeat in the past does not
prove that self-victory doesn't exist.

The only thing a thousand failed
attempts to start your life over
prove is that you just started in the
wrong place a thousand times.

Trying to start our life over
because we want to get away
from our sad self—or the sorry
situations it has created—is like
leaping onto a sinking ship to
get off a collapsing dock.

Letting go is all about finding
out who you are not and having
the courage to leave it at that.

The only reason that any pain
from our past persists is because
there is something in us that
won't let it die out naturally.

Just as a weary rock climber must at
times reach above himself to gain a
difficult resting ledge, you too must
dare to go beyond yourself to find this
ever-present safety. There is no danger
in true self-ascent. The only real danger
lies within remaining where you are.

In this new life, every relationship
begins for the first time over and
over again. Every discouragement
is over, right now. Every challenge,
every difficulty is shouldered only in
its time and is *never* carried forward
or looked back upon with regret.
Isn't that what all of us really want?

You are so much more
than you can think.

Just as who you really are is
not created to be limited or
defined by your present way of
feeling, neither must you look
for who you really are in your
thoughts about yourself.

Any painful past moment must pass
the moment you lose interest in it!

Drop angry and anxious
feelings instantly.

In itself, real higher understanding
supplies you with everything
you need to actualize it:
clarity, instruction, and
encouragement to succeed.

Give up self-righteousness.
It only feels like something right.
It is coming from something that
is wrong. Right isn't something
you feel; it is something you are.

Give up anger toward
others and yourself.
See that the force of any heated
reaction is not strength. Remember
that for any and every action
of force, there is an equal and
opposite one. This explains why
the fighting never ends. Let it end.

Give up self-torment.
It drives you—but it doesn't take
you anywhere. Who you really are
never suffers over who you are not.

As you begin to suspend your habitual
involvement with yourself—which
you know you must do in order to let
something new happen—you begin to
notice an altogether different kind of
disturbing feeling starting to rise up
within you: *you are actually beginning to worry
about what is going to happen to you without your
worry.* Nothing doing! You instantly
catch and drop this fake feeling, along
with the rest of the inner impostors.

Don't let the current of the
past dictate the direction of
the present moment. Have
your own life right now.

You are not your thoughts and feelings. Dare to live without each painful identity that calls for you to embrace it and do its bidding. Let something new happen each moment by letting these old, habitual sensations go their way unobstructed. Stay out of them.

No human being has any authority over you. Your life belongs to you and to you alone. No scowling face or irritated manner, no challenging posture or threatening tone, has any power to make you feel nervous or anxious, frightened or angry.

No human being has any authority
over who you really are. Your
true nature answers to no one.

Being approved of by others has
become a strange kind of life-support
system wherein, after a lifetime of
depending on it, you unconsciously
believe that there won't be life without
someone there to approve you into
existence. Just the opposite is true.
The more you depend on others
to confirm you to yourself, the less
real life you have of your own.

Imagine a murky countryside pond. It could have a depth of several fathoms, or it could be just knee deep. Inner difficulties only *seem* deep because our false nature keeps everything so stirred up inside of us that we can't see to the real bottom of them.

When we are inwardly quiet
and can see ourselves clearly,
we can wade through our
difficulties without any fear
of being in over our heads.

The chief cause of why our lives
so often wind up in the hands of
others is not that they are superior
or that the world is too strong for
us, but that we don't want to face
the uncertainty and aloneness we
think we are too weak to bear.

The conscious refusal to go along
with what your weakness wants you
to do to escape its uncertainty is
what invokes and finally delivers
real inner confidence. This new
kind of strength gradually becomes
the cornerstone of a true individual
existence—the life you've always wanted.

If you will stay in the middle of this struggle for true self-possession, not asserting your individuality but allowing it to flourish and to blossom—bearing what you must bear by refusing to submit yourself to negative, self-betraying influences—you will come to know the highest approval that life can award: reality itself will approve you.

The more approval you get,
the more you have to have.

Keeping any person or
circumstance in your life
that demands you surrender
your right to be a whole and
happy human being is wrong
for everyone involved.

When you are out standing in a storm, don't blame the weather.

As shocking as it may seem at
first to learn, most of the people
around you don't want you to
wake up and have your own life.

No one really wants to talk about it, but the truth is, there is a kind of "evil spell" hanging over each of us and our world as well. In fact, part of this global spell is our denial of its existence. It is called suffering. Everyone believes that their suffering somehow benefits them. That's how the spell works.

Negative emotions feel like they are in your best interest because, at the time of their intrusion into your life, they temporarily fill you with a powerful false sense of self. However, this sense of self born out of fierce but lying feelings can only exist without your conscious consent or awareness of its being there.

Listening to your own mind give
you "good reasons" why you should
be fearful over unexpected events
is just like being friends with
someone who thinks it's funny
to find new ways to hurt you!

The only way that any suffering
feeling can prove to you that
you need it is to hypnotize
you with a flood of itself.
Step back from yourself.

Suffering doesn't prove that you know what it means to care about yourself or others. What it does prove is you haven't seen through your own ideas about caring or you wouldn't be so careless with yourself.

Suffering doesn't prove that you are right. What it does prove is you don't really know right from wrong or you wouldn't take your position of pain as your proof of point.

Suffering doesn't prove that you are responsible. What it does prove is you have abandoned true self-responsibility or you wouldn't treat yourself so badly.

Suffering doesn't prove that you are important. What it does prove is you would rather feel like a "someone" who is miserable than be a "no one" who is free and quietly happy.

Suffering doesn't prove that you
are all alone in life. What it does
prove is you prefer the company of
unfriendly thoughts and feelings
whose very nature is to isolate
you from everything good.

Suffering doesn't prove that the world is against you. What it does prove is you have taken sides with that which is against everything—including yourself.

Suffering doesn't prove that you are real. What it does prove is you have identified with an agitated false feeling of life and confused it for the quiet fullness of real living.

Suffering doesn't prove that someone else is wrong. What it does prove is you will go to any lengths, including self-destruction, to prove that you are right.

Suffering doesn't prove that you are who you think you are. What it does prove is you don't know who you really are or you would never tolerate a suffering self as an identity.

Suffering over your suffering doesn't prove you want to stop suffering. What it does prove is you are afraid of the end of suffering because you think the end of it means the end of you. It does not.

You do not have to accept
any inner condition that
compromises your happiness.

The next time you catch yourself
starting to feel bad about anything,
immediately stop everything you are
doing for a moment and, as simply
and as honestly as you can, ask
yourself: "Is this what I really want?"

You can and must inwardly say to
any conflicting thoughts or feelings
that "you are not what I want!" The
clearer this whole picture becomes
to you—that suffering is stupid
and must never be justified—the
stronger your right self-assertion
for self-unity will become.

Stop worrying about who you think you *should* be, and start being who you are. How? Stop telling yourself who you should be, and start listening for an altogether new kind of voice that has been quietly calling to you.

Dare to walk away from all of
the familiar but useless mental
and emotional relationships
that give you a temporary but
unsatisfactory sense of self.

Your true identity is calling to you.
But to hear it you must be willing
to endure, for as long as necessary,
the fear of self-uncertainty.

The only thing certain about fear
is that it will *always* compromise
you. When it comes to who you
really are, there is *no* compromise.

True newness in life is more than just a self-pleasing notion. It becomes our experience of life each time we choose to let go and live without allowing who we have been in the past to tell us who we must be in the present moment.

Learn to consciously question those parts of yourself that would have you believe life is made meaningful by how much you suffer over it.

Our wish to understand and
dismiss any dark shadow that
wants to overcome us awakens
within us a living light that sees
to it our wish comes true.

The fear of being alone is born
out of keeping company with parts
of yourself that want you to feel
incomplete so that they can lead
you into one self-compromising
relationship after another!

Mostly unanswered but endlessly calling to each and every one of us is our natural and higher need to find our place in the sun; a world just outside of our old, limited self where real life is open and free. This need in each of us to rise above ourselves is an eternal law expressing itself in all living things.

The wise eagle knows just where
to wait on the winds for certain
powerful updrafts. Its compliance
with natural laws is rewarded with
a soaring life. So too must we learn
to comply with the higher laws that
govern self-liberation if we wish to
be lifted above our present self.

Surely you have felt the need for a greater life outside of yourself. Who hasn't? We all feel this natural need for rising above self-limiting thoughts and feelings because our true nature, like the light that is its source, beckons us to emerge from under the heaviness of our own mistaken false identity.

Here's the most important thing to remember whenever you find yourself in a mad rush: what you really want, what you're really after, is a quiet mind—a peaceable state of self reached only by realizing there is no place more empowering for you to be than in the present moment.

Your faint but sincere wish
to leave your false self behind
compels the lower nature to do
everything in its power to make
you believe that self-exit is not
only dangerous but impossible.

The false self and all that makes it up
is *mechanical* in nature. It is made up of
dusty memories, conditioned beliefs,
habitual associations, ancient fears,
recurring doubts, familiar pleasures,
and many other reactions of endless
variety. In short, the false self is not
really alive. It has no more real life than
does a fifty-cent amusement park ride.

Every sustained effort you make
to grow beyond yourself—to help
effect a real change in your present
level of consciousness—brings
up in you a host of negative
thoughts and feelings that can't
wait to point out the negatives
as to why this can't be done.

Remember that inner progress is
not measured by what you do with
any scary thoughts or feelings,
but by how well you understand
this new instruction: there is
nothing that needs to be done
with any dark state, except for
you to stay awake and watchful.

The journey outside of yourself
doesn't take you to a place, but
to the realization that who you
really are lives above the world
of thoughts and feelings.

Nothing stands between you
and permanent happiness.

The only path to self-
success is your next step.

No one else can help you
get outside of yourself, but
you must let everyone show
you the need to do so.

Real success is not measured
by what you are driven to
achieve but by what you can
quietly understand.

Giving your consent to live in
fear of some moment to come
is no different than walking out
of the warm sunlight into a dark
shadow … and then blaming the
sun for your sudden chill.

If there is suffering in your
heart, it is only because you
have mistaken an unwanted
intruder for an invited guest.

The up-and-down/down-and-up movement of our emotional life is not real life any more than waves are all there is to an ocean.

Give yourself permission to be
just as dissatisfied as you really
are with what your present
level of life provides for you.

Our feelings of unhappiness
and incompleteness aren't born
out of how life has treated us
but rather by what we have
been calling life. Anger,
disappointment, and frustration,
or any of their skyrocketing
opposites, are only sensations.

Calling our up-and-down feelings "real life" doesn't make them so, any more than calling a kitchen blender an airplane makes it capable of flight just because it hums and vibrates!

As you walk away from your own self-generated inner life, you will begin to discover that all of the sensations you thought were giving you life were actually separating you from it.

The truth is that each of life's terrifying mountain passes, filled with all of its unknown hostiles, is an inner affair.

The way out is safe. You are protected in a way that you cannot think about. In fact, you mustn't think at all about the "dangers" of walking away from yourself. Instead, you must see the endangered "you" that your thinking creates!

The real danger lies not with
the unexpected but with
remaining where you are in
your present life-level.

We succeed in this life when—no matter win or lose in the eyes of the world—we can walk away from any demanding moment with a measure of more true self-understanding than we took into it.

The true spiritual warrior
knows the only enemy she has
is what she has yet to shed light
upon in herself; therefore,
she never postpones a battle
that must be engaged.

The true spiritual warrior starts
life over, over and over again.

The true spiritual warrior works
every day, every moment, to
sharpen her battle skills.

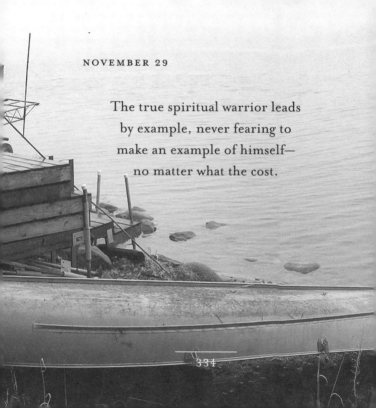

The true spiritual warrior leads
by example, never fearing to
make an example of himself—
no matter what the cost.

The true spiritual warrior is
never afraid to look at what
she doesn't want to see.

The true spiritual warrior commits
himself to his best choice and
realizes that to live in conflict
over what is or is not best is
the refusal of responsibility.

The true spiritual warrior never fears feelings of helplessness, because she recognizes such states as the heralds of new powers to come, like storm clouds before spring flowers.

The true spiritual warrior
knows that the path of spiritual
liberation that he has chosen
must lead him to one encounter
after another with conditions that
always seem greater than he is.

Ask which you would rather do:
temporarily subdue a painful
personal problem and live with
the knowledge that you will
have to fight with it again one
day, or let go of that unhappy
condition altogether by seeing
through it to its actual cause.

We are learning that what appears
to be legions of impossible
difficulties is actually nothing but
an army of dark imaginings—and
that these troubled thoughts and
feelings of ours are the only forces
that keep us from having and
enjoying life on our own terms.

Unlike living in the outer world, where being with others cannot be avoided, in the inner world just the opposite is true. Inwardly there is nothing that can stop us from being alone, and that is our ultimate victory over harmful voices and scary feelings: they must have our ear or they have no one to talk to.

Start today—right now—the practice of living alone within yourself. If you persist with this kind of watchfulness, then one day the word "alone" won't frighten you anymore, and here's why: there will be no more dark thoughts left within your psychic system to talk to you about how lonely you feel.

You must never hesitate to see through people, nor should you ever feel guilty for what your awakening perception reveals to you about them. This guilty feeling, as if you've done something bad by seeing badness in others, is a trick of the false self. It needs to keep you believing in others so that later on you can feel stressed and betrayed when they fail to live up to your expectations.

You can only depend on others
for as long as it pays them to
tolerate your dependence.

Depending on others for
a sense of independent
psychological well-being is an
accident waiting to happen.

Don't be afraid to come to the
temporarily disturbing but
wonderful understanding that
there is no one for you to count
on, because there isn't—at least
not where you have been looking.

Unbeknownst to yourself, you have been living with the self-limiting belief that one day someone will give you what you haven't been able to give to yourself—true independence. Well, the wait is over and so is the fear.

It isn't in another's power to do
for you what you must do for
yourself. It never has been.

Stop looking for what you *hope* to
see in others, and start seeing what
you *need* to see to help set you free.

Before you turn to another person
for help, honestly see if he has
ever really helped himself. Look
for his wings, not at his words.

When you understand that no
one really knows who they are,
you will stop looking to them
to tell you who you are.

Neither the approval nor the disapproval of any individual or group makes any real difference in the quality of your life.

Why do you want the approval
of those who don't even
approve of themselves?

One way to avoid at least a few
unpleasant conversations is
to stop talking to yourself!

Ninety-nine people can approve
of you, but if the one-hundredth
scowls, your day is ruined.

If you are headed
for the mountaintop,
why do you care
what the people in
the valley are doing?

Someone with all the knowledge
in the world, but who can't
understand the need to sacrifice
his selfish little "self" for the
sake of a greater kindness, is no
different than a donkey with a
whole library strapped to its back.

Only wrongness needs to check
with itself to see if it's right.

Stop trying to act kindly and dare
to be more awake, for the kindest
act of all is to help another see
through the hoax of unhappiness.

As long as you act as though
your life depends upon
anything temporal, it does.

Your secret strength knows
that your secret weakness
isn't yours at all.

False life is exhausting;
real life is inexhaustible.

Any confidence you may have based
on something outside yourself is
also the basis of your self-doubt.

If you allow others to tell you where
you are going, then you must also
depend on them to tell you what
you will need for your journey.

The Secret Self knows the frustration in our demands and wisely instructs us to accept the relief and release that comes with wanting what it wants.

The Secret Self knows the anguish
of our attachments and assures us
that letting go of what we think we
must have to be happy is the same
as letting go of our unhappiness.

A Special Gift for You:
Free 60-Minute DVD by Guy Finley
To Touch the Timeless Mind

The quality of your life—for better or worse—is determined by one thing: the level of your consciousness. Raise your consciousness, and you will raise the quality of your whole life!

· You will be a more profitable person.

· You will have better relationships.

· You will have fewer problems.

· You will be a better friend and parent.

· You will enjoy a more enlightened life.

In this powerful, free 60-minute DVD by Guy Finley, gain the wisdom to *let go* of what limits you.*

Visit www.guyfinley.org/newDVD

or call (541) 476-1200

to request your **FREE** DVD today!

* Offer includes free shipping to U.S. addresses only. Limited time offer. Subject to change. Please see web site for further information and restrictions.